Iowa *simply beautiful*

photography by Larsh K. Bristol, Curt Maas *and others*

American & World Geographic Publishing

Above: Pot of gold in Johnston. CURT MAAS

Title page: Winter windbreak. CURT MAAS

Front cover: Emerald and chocolate in the middle of soybean season. CURT MAAS

Back cover: Aaah, yes, it's Iowa—near Waterville. LARSH K. BRISTOL

ISBN: 1-56037-160-9
© 2000 American & World Geographic Publishing
Photography © 2000 Larsh K. Bristol, Curt Maas, Tom Bean and James Blank
This book may not be reproduced in whole or in part by any means (with the exception of short quotes for the purpose of review) without permission of the publisher. For more information on our books call or write: American & World Geographic Publishing, P.O. Box 5630, Helena, Montana 59604, (406) 443-2842 or (800) 654-1105.
Book catalog appears online at www.montanamagazine.com/books
Printed in Hong Kong

FOREWORD

When I travel outside the midwest on assignment and answer where I'm from, many people then say, "Iowa, huh?...I guess they grow a lot of potatoes there, don't they?" obviously mistaking Iowa for Idaho. I have to chuckle to myself a little, and explain, "No, they don't grow a lot of potatoes but they sure do raise a lot of corn, soybeans and pork!"

While this may be true, I have always noticed Iowa as being a rural, scenic landscape with a beauty all its own. Once you get off the main highways and interstates you'll find Iowa to be a landscape with farmsteads, grazing cattle, crops of mostly corn and soybeans, creeks, rivers, lakes, parks, gravel roads, and of course, small towns. Lots of small towns.

Even though Iowa has its metropolitan areas, I think the small towns are what give the state its overall personality. People are always friendly and helpful, and you can still stop for lunch at a local cafe and get a hearty meal that's just like homemade.

As I travel around on gravel roads I can't help but notice some of the old weathered barns that still dot the countryside. It makes me wonder what life must have been like in the early part of the 20th century before electricity, hot and cold running water, and all of the other conveniences we take for granted today.

Agriculture has always been a large part of Iowa's life and its economy, and the people who farm the land are some of the nicest, most sincere people you can meet anywhere. I also think farmers are the "artists" of the landscape. As they work the land with all of their equipment, they're creating an array of shapes, patterns, textures, and colors, that can best be appreciated when you're flying in a small airplane a thousand or so feet overhead. It's a quilted patchwork of sorts, changing as the seasons change.

Extremes of weather also affect anyone who has lived in Iowa for a while. From spring rains, high winds, and a tornado or two in the summer, to the sub-zero wind chills, snowfall and blizzards in the winter, it seems like a reminder to the soul of what you can't control, and how furious Mother Nature can be at times. It also renews your faith in a "higher power." But Iowa has its share of great weather, too. When the conditions are right, you won't find more spectacular sunsets or sunrises anywhere, and I feel very privileged to be able to capture them on film.

One other very significant thing about Iowa is the changing of the seasons. If you ask anyone who has lived here what they would miss about Iowa, most will say it's just that. From barren ground to budding trees and flowers in the spring, into the rich green shades of growing crops during the summer, then transforming into the fiery golds of autumn, and back to a white, snow-covered landscape during winter, each season displays its own beautiful effect on Iowa.

As a photographer, I hope I've been able to capture some of these beauties. I hope these images make you want to get off the beaten path sometime and travel the back roads to experience Iowa's simple beauty for yourself.

—*Curt Maas*

Born and raised in Northeast Iowa, I (like so many other teens) could not wait to get somewhere else—there was a whole world out there to explore and conquer.

I went west to college and stayed. For fifteen years I worked as a photojournalist, learning my craft, honing my skills and, except for family, not thinking much about my home state.

That all changed when I came "home" to document the mid-1980s farm crisis that nearly bankrupted the entire Midwest. Thinking that I would only be in Iowa for, at the most, six months, I looked forward to living next to family and old friends, but knew I'd return to the mountains and endless vistas of my adopted state of Wyoming.

Then something happened. I saw a state I had never taken the time to see while growing up. I discovered the beauty of the verdant rolling hills covered with vibrant hardwood forests that turn brilliant colors in fall and stand proud and bare all winter. Fresh, rushing trout streams that empty into rivers carved from towering limestone bluffs past Indian burial mounds, abandoned mills, and people of all ages fishing from boat or bank hoping to catch a dinner of trout, bass, or walleye.

Iowa produces one fifth of the United States corn crop. CURT MAAS

There is natural beauty in Iowa which I hope this book portrays. There is also man-made beauty: contoured corn fields, golden tassels dancing in the sun, sunflowers reaching for a clear blue sky, lush green alfalfa waving in a summer breeze. But I hope viewers of this book also notice Iowa's best natural asset—its people. I can't begin to describe the strong work ethic, love of fun, and friendliness of Iowa people. There's a contentment there—a peace, if you will, of knowing where you belong.

Iowa may not have 12,000-foot peaks or mile-deep gorges, but we can look over amber fields of grain and know that we help feed the world and there is a good feeling in that.

Iowa is my home once again. It's the same Iowa I grew up in, but I've changed and see the beauty now that some may seem to miss. I hope this book shows you Iowa isn't all flat—or all cornfields, or all farmers. Although my work takes me traveling throughout the world, I always look forward to coming home to Iowa.

—*Larsh K. Bristol*

Getting the load in before a storm hits, near Westfield. TOM BEAN

Facing page: Serious about fly fishing on Bear Creek. LARSH K. BRISTOL

With the Civil War slowing things down, the first rail line entered Iowa from the east in 1856, but did not extend across the Missouri until 1867. LARSH K. BRISTOL

Facing page: Getting in some cool-weather kayaking below Bald Eagle. LARSH K. BRISTOL

Soybeans and corn—mainstays of Iowa agriculture. CURT MAAS

Rolling hills of the heartland. CURT MAAS

Left: I'm not ready for market yet—how 'bout you? CURT MAAS

Below: An ocean of storm over central Iowa. CURT MAAS

Facing page: Autumn comes chilling down. CURT MAAS

Monarch butterfly visits a garden zinnia. CURT MAAS

Left: With sixty insurance companies headquartered here, Des Moines is the world's third-largest insurance center. CURT MAAS

The Upper Iowa River's Lower Dam. LARSH K. BRISTOL

Facing page: Harvest time in the Elon area. LARSH K. BRISTOL

Near Booneville, the silver gleam of a grain train means green for farmers' pockets. CURT MAAS

Left: It may be simple, but it's my home. CURT MAAS

Below: Effigy Mounds National Monument, near Harpers Ferry, recalls the Mound Builder Indians who walked this land beginning more than two millennia ago. LARSH K. BRISTOL

Frigid winter sunset. CURT MAAS

Midwestern grain on its way to market, down the Father of Waters. LARSH K. BRISTOL

Grain co-op manager Howard Berkley pauses to enjoy a rewarding view. LARSH K. BRISTOL

It was a hot, sticky uphill ride near Cumming for the 1997 RAGBRAI (Register's Annual Great Bike Ride Across Iowa). CURT MAAS

Dutch Calvinists seeking religious freedom founded Pella in 1847. JAMES BLANK

Sunset near Benton City. CURT MAAS

Facing page: Passing isn't necessary when you get up early enough to have the road all to yourself. CURT MAAS

Fresh snow adds beauty to a cold Iowa morning. CURT MAAS

Facing page: Your wish is my command. CURT MAAS

Nearly pure (23 karat) gold leaf shines atop the Iowa capitol's main dome, high above Des Moines. TOM BEAN

Pikes Peak State Park is named for explorer Zebulon Pike, who explored the Upper Mississippi in 1805-1806, and named 14,110-foot Pikes Peak in Colorado the following year. TOM BEAN

Early green corn near Audubon. CURT MAAS

A brand-new soybean plant sprouts. CURT MAAS

Autumn is bursting out along quiet Mississippi backwaters. LARSH K. BRISTOL

Angus-Hereford steaks of the future. LARSH K. BRISTOL

Facing page: Prosperous parents gave their children this unusual early-20th century one-room schoolhouse, with bell tower. LARSH K. BRISTOL

Left: Cattail art. CURT MAAS

Far left: Near Garner in Hancock County. CURT MAAS

Below: Waukon's former courthouse now serves as a museum. CURT MAAS

Right: The magic time of day. LARSH K. BRISTOL

Below: Spring bursts into southeast Iowa. LARSH K. BRISTOL

Sunset sentinels. LARSH K. BRISTOL

Facing page: Strolling through the woodland cathedral. LARSH K. BRISTOL

Right: Straight as an arrow, blacktop races across the countryside. CURT MAAS

Below: Sandpipers feeding in the shallows of a western Iowa waterway. CURT MAAS

Lookout tower lends a certain air to the autumn mood in Backbone State Park. TOM BEAN

Saying farewell to a friend at a horse sale.
LARSH K. BRISTOL

Right: A substantial investment in north-east Iowa. LARSH K. BRISTOL

Above: As boys in McGregor, the five young Ringling Brothers practiced circus-producing skills that later made their fortunes. TOM BEAN

Right: It's a serious business, delivering milk. LARSH K. BRISTOL

Facing page: View from the bluffs in Pikes Peak State Park. LARSH K. BRISTOL

A sight to worry a farmer right in the middle of corn season. CURT MAAS

Facing page: Will the holiday snow begin tomorrow in West Des Moines? TOM BEAN

Snowmelt flows into Beaver Creek. CURT MAAS

Above: An inspiring view of New Albion.
LARSH K. BRISTOL

Right: Following the pheasant in new-fallen snow. CURT MAAS

A canoe flotilla descends on Marquette. LARSH K. BRISTOL

Facing page: Peaceful, pastoral, and stirring. LARSH K. BRISTOL

Left: Patriotic greeting. CURT MAAS

Below: Central Iowa from the mid-season summer sky. CURT MAAS

Fall patterns near Dorchester. CURT MAAS

Glacier-carved Lake Okoboji, Iowa's deepest lake, provides one of the state's popular resort areas. JAMES BLANK

Facing page: Tallgrass prairie has been restored to its original state—with plants like these black-eyed Susans and wildlife including buffalo—at Neal Smith National Wildlife Refuge near Prairie City. TOM BEAN

Left: Spring rains leave their mark. CURT MAAS

Below: Bounty of the harvest at Granger. CURT MAAS

Roseman covered bridge, southwest of Winterset in Madison County. TOM BEAN

Facing page: Summer kettle drums tuning up? LARSH K. BRISTOL

Blackhawk Bridge connects Lansing to western Wisconsin. LARSH K. BRISTOL

White egret ballet. LARSH K. BRISTOL

Celebrating harvest-time at Amana. TOM BEAN

Facing page: Storm's end at Loess Hills State Forest near Pisgah. TOM BEAN

Above: The palette of autumn hardwoods. LARSH K. BRISTOL

Below: Sometimes it's not the snowfall that gets you—it's the wind afterward, as here near Des Moines.
CURT MAAS

A study in winter tones. CURT MAAS

Leading edge of a cold front moving in from Nebraska. CURT MAAS

Dusk falls over Davenport, and the Centennial Bridge lights the way. JAMES BLANK

The beauty of dew on a garden spider's web. CURT MAAS

Left: A mystical and misty day near Waterville. LARSH K. BRISTOL

Thank you, but I'd really rather go this way. LARSH K. BRISTOL

Twin Springs in northeastern Iowa offer a cool place on a hot summer day. LARSH K. BRISTOL

Early-morning river traffic on the Mississippi. LARSH K. BRISTOL

The talkin' and the jokin' may beat the fishin' when old friends get together. LARSH K. BRISTOL

After harvest near Vincent in Webster County. CURT MAAS

Sunset promises a good day tomorrow, near Dallas Center. CURT MAAS

Tasseled symmetry near Harlan. CURT MAAS

Looking across to the Wisconsin bluffs from Heytmans Landing, once a wood stop for Mississippi steamboats.
LARSH K. BRISTOL

Morning mist and an awakening landscape. CURT MAAS

Four skis and four legs out for a winter stroll in Yellow River State Forest. LARSH K. BRISTOL

A sturdy reminder of frontier hope in northeast Iowa. LARSH K. BRISTOL

Facing page: For all the problems ice storms bring, they also are beautiful. LARSH K. BRISTOL

Hot and hazy at Clear Lake. LARSH K. BRISTOL

Right: To many, foxtail is a weed, but to a photographer it can be a work of art. CURT MAAS

Below: Allamakee County in the northeast is bordered by the Mississippi River and Minnesota. LARSH K. BRISTOL

Just after the storm, near Mt. Pleasant. CURT MAAS

Early breath of autumn on the eastern border. CURT MAAS

A study in angles: Lansing's historical architecture seen through Blackhawk Bridge. LARSH K. BRISTOL

Facing page: Winter's red, white, and blue. LARSH K. BRISTOL

Aerial view of the Loess Hills north of Sioux City. TOM BEAN

Facing page: Grist mill and dam dating from 1848 are preserved at Wildcat Den State Park near Muscatine. JAMES BLANK

Right: Another of autumn's many joys!
LARSH K. BRISTOL

Below: The twenty-sixth state in size, mighty Iowa supplies seven percent of the U.S.'s food. LARSH K. BRISTOL

Algona, seat of Kossuth County, presents a tidy view from the sky. CURT MAAS

The wild rose may be Iowa's state flower, but sunflowers are the very presence of summer.
LARSH K. BRISTOL

Left: A Cumming barn suitable for a painting.
CURT MAAS

Right: A good catch of panfish on the farm pond. CURT MAAS

Below: Crows add contrast on a frosty day. CURT MAAS

Facing page: Fit for a holiday greeting card. LARSH K. BRISTOL

The red of sugar maples is one of autumn's delights. LARSH K. BRISTOL

Facing page: Gentle rain, gentle rainbow. LARSH K. BRISTOL

Storm Lake, between Sioux City and Fort Dodge, is a haven for water sports and outdoor recreation. JAMES BLANK

Facing page: Off to a solid start. LARSH K. BRISTOL

The Mississippi flood of 1993, seen here, caused $2 billion in damage to Iowa, but it also enriched land for the future. LARSH K. BRISTOL

Dangerous beauty on a summer day. TOM BEAN

Right: A dairy herd on the job, interrupted by the fellow with that clicking black box. LARSH K. BRISTOL

Below: Storm warning for Sioux City! LARSH K. BRISTOL

Facing page: The Upper Iowa River still carves patiently through confining limestone. LARSH K. BRISTOL

Competition dancing at an Iowa powwow. LARSH K. BRISTOL

Stretching the day to bring in the soybean harvest. CURT MAAS

Getting washed and pretty for the Bigger and Better Allamakee County Fair. LARSH K. BRISTOL

Below: A proud designation on the Sam Kellogg farm near Percival. LARSH K. BRISTOL

Facing page: Autumn splendor near Decorah. JAMES BLANK

Evening pastels over the corncrib, central Iowa. CURT MAAS

Left: Corn silk just waiting for the pollen delivery. CURT MAAS

Below: An inviting summer find. CURT MAAS

The Mississippi, placid under autumn's enameled sky. LARSH K. BRISTOL

Above: Light and darkness reverse under a storm-tossed sky.
LARSH K. BRISTOL

Right: Sunset and moonrise over Saylorville Lake's mile-long bridge. CURT MAAS

Right: Yellow River as its namesake state forest turns yellow. LARSH K. BRISTOL

Below: Dairy farm with a view, near Harpers Ferry. CURT MAAS

Under the railroad bridge at Bluffton, Upper Iowa River. LARSH K. BRISTOL

Born with the twentieth century, near Woodward. CURT MAAS

A quiet stroll through a city park in Spencer. CURT MAAS

Dallas Center's elevators awaiting this year's crop. CURT MAAS

Nothing beats canoeing on a crisp autumn day. LARSH K. BRISTOL

Right: That'd be a man who enjoys his work.
LARSH K. BRISTOL

Below: Quick—a place to hide! LARSH K. BRISTOL

A sub-zero day in central Iowa. CURT MAAS